AN ENGRAVED WOMAN

poems by

JENQUIA JAMISON

Finishing Line Press
Georgetown, Kentucky

AN ENGRAVED WOMAN

Copyright © 2023 by Jenquia Jamison
ISBN 979-8-88838-221-9 First Edition
All rights reserved under International and Pan-American Copyright Conventions. No part of this book may be reproduced in any manner whatsoever without written permission from the publisher, except in the case of brief quotations embodied in critical articles and reviews.

ACKNOWLEDGMENTS

Thank you to all of my family, friends and co-works who gave a listening ear with feedback each time I shared my poetry. I would also like to thank Finishing Line Press for making this possible and most importantly, Yahwey.

Publisher: Leah Huete de Maines
Editor: Christen Kincaid
Cover Art and Illustrator: Jenquia Jamison
Author Photo: Photographer Cammy Neal
Cover Design: Elizabeth Maines McCleavy

Order online: www.finishinglinepress.com
also available on amazon.com

Author inquiries and mail orders:
Finishing Line Press
PO Box 1626
Georgetown, Kentucky 40324
USA

Table of Contents

Speak 1

Cigarette Burnz 2

A Sudden Touch 3

Love Disrupted 4

Does He 6

A Battle with Love 7

Goodbye Luv 9

A Seated State 10

A Child's Temptation 11

Cocaine 12

Girl Lost 13

A Place Of Desolate 15

Not Another Statistic 16

Unsettled 18

I Love and Hate My Hair 19

Glide Jelly Bean Glide 20

Finding Beauty 21

Timeless Dream 22

He Kisses My Acne 23

A Mind That Soon Sleeps 24

Remember Me 25

I dedicate this chapbook to every woman who has felt burdens life can sometimes leave behind. This collection of poems was written not just for me, but for you as well to say your voice matters and despite what the world tells you, you are beautiful. As women, we are a collection of many things battered, bruised, ignored and shamed. I tell you now, no matter what belittling title the world wants to give you, we are indomitable, and I celebrate us all.

SPEAK

Speak to me in a manner unvexed
leaving no void for questions unanswered
The truth you hold was never meant to be complex
And without honesty, there will never be a next
A next rise; a next mind of elevation…
For without it is to walk with a tongue of lies drowning in damnation

Speak to me with your heart and let your mind carry your words
displaying characteristics of nobility, dependability and spiritually
open at its most sincerity
This is your voice-Speak!
Not just today but all days of the week

Begin a new day living in a new way with words unfolded away from
false pretense
Allow the stages of baptizing to commence
As you walk in truth; the true you will finally live again
Speak

CIGARETTE BURNZ

My first occurrence of ashes to my skin
was a kindred touch
Little did I know it would convey a distress
from childhood to grownup
Detesting the very thing that should have been my protector
I died that night laid out like human remains on a stretcher
Daddy wasn't there
Couldn't call for God as I didn't know prayer
No solace Or guidance
alone with a lifetime of silence
Washing myself never erased the violence
So Smoke filled my air
As ashes timely scattered
Cigarette burns abraded my flesh
I cried leaving my face a mess
realizing my body nor life ever mattered

The second encounter
was given in the gentlest touch from skin to skin
What was disguised as love
was a forever transmission of a
lifetime of pain, mistrust, and prescriptions
These wounds on my skin will not heal and are forming blisters
I now walk
lost in a hellish storm of raging twisters
Bitter treats un-sweetened
came in all forms of people
What is left of me now
is the heart of someone badly weakened
So don't tell me I can't smoke
Who cares if my lungs fill up until I choke
Life laughed at me the day I was born
Now Cigarette Burnz are the only marks I know

A SUDDEN TOUCH

It advents as a string of pearls unhurriedly Or swiftly wafting through the air
Like a lightning strike to ones back
with sonorous movements as a car speaker's bass to my spine
I am acquired off guard
Caught in a fisher's net
with the look of trepidation affixed upon my face
Its force to my shoulder has displace
the skin that stood in its place
When I turn from looking away,
will I feel agreeably to this sudden touch
in an alluring Or repelling way
What solace will await
Or will treachery be at play

Nerves arouse with scatter
As my teeth starts to chatter
but no sound comes out
There is a rumbling within my stomach
As my feet thinks to take flight
Have I been met by a breeze on a succulent summer night
Or have I been thwacked by deciding hands out of spite
What gladdening this could be if all goes right
Or
What tragedy may accompany me as darkness sex's the night

LOVE DISRUPTED

A smiling face I once held
with balanced walks and a heart compelled
I probed for love in the blackest hell
It drizzled my tongue with a savor of stale

Unchanging waves came pummeling in
My heart was wavered at deaths end
Endless nights I breathe within
with tarnished nails and honed tins

To rest angst adjoined by weeps
Alive yet immobile with walking feet
 Brawny lungs and vocals that bolster speech
 In expired silence I cannot speak

I cried a tale of tethered sheep's
From buffeted storms and a death too deep
I sleep now abutting a bristled touch
with bleeding holes from cupid's clutch

I reclined my hands to you outwardly
Pulling back hollowed air and smut
What emerged back was only me
as your skin to mine was never touched

Manic reflections pour out from me
I've withered fast into decay
Once a flower bloomed from seed
Now on deserted roads I walk astray
with wandering thoughts to oneself
how ugly the day must have felt
when momma's womb birthed
an empty shell

As boomerangs,
downcast inevitably comes back to me
with piercing sounds of screeching nails
and frowned up noses from a carcass smell
I dread the moment life gave yell
As my first birthing sound when darkness dwelled

No dreams or visions with future hopes
Just wounded lungs from a deadly choke
Distorted images from a painter's brush
of an uncle's love unpleasant in touch
My heart beats as a battered drum

Can life go back reversed in time?
Before seeds are splattered
And rain is gathered
Before clouded skies hovered light
And happy kids played with kites

Reality settles with horrific weather
I crumble about as plucked feathers
No winds to raise my feet together
Will I ever escape?
I think,
Never

DOES HE

Does he wrap you gently with the softest arms
Or hold tightly until your skin becomes black and blue?

Does he mirror the image of a wholesome man
Or speaks of it without intent?

When your face is lit with the most captivating smile, is his Or
does he instantly turn your happy upside down?

When you are alone with closed eyes,
do you recap memories of the love he kept
Or dream with imagination of what your heart has yet felt?

Are you afraid to speak?
Afraid to…Be
You as You are, not the outer surface but deeply

Does he treat your thoughts as nothing to hear Or engage activity
with listening ears?

Does he compliment your spirit Or
is He Of the worldly man's dreams of a
dime piece having nothing past the physical?

Can you share your inner most fears and know comfort is always
near or sit with a silent tongue awaiting your grand premiere?

A BATTLE WITH LOVE

While I ponder
your existence to mine,
there is a dissatisfaction
of monogamy embedded in fractions
with timeless pieces of my heart
fed to a walking corpse
I can't un-taste this bitter waste
Blackberry molasses was your favorite of choice,
beauty to the eyes but unflavored to the soul

You arrived as a tidal wave killing all
in its way
No starlight's or shiny days
Smiles kept a distance away
My seat is not at a child's place
where kids play
I sit head,
not for fun,
But to absorb all these bullets
you steadily shoot my way
Waging my love in a cards game,
unaware of my magnificent hands
My title as Queen without king,
I still reclaim

The pressure of my feet is GRAND
Grand! Meaning
When I walk, all things slam
Every door
Every window
Every inanimate object explodes into nano pieces
As the stain of you and what you stood for
steadily decreases
I choose to un-battle this

So,
watch your hands carefully
since you couldn't care for me
Listen for the sound of a snake's hiss
Or be met dreadfully
with a black widow's kiss

GOODBYE LUV

Confusion should be the name of Love's game
made of distorted images and spoken-less words which are really
illusions from a delusional mind
I am sick of pointless intrusions
while I give open-hearted music,
My ears are struck with silence and a lack of movement
Thought I'd give in and try some new shit
but each day, I am sickened by lames I cannot be enthused with
when I am what others should want to be infused with
So, you win Love. I give up.
My body can't handle another wound or bruising.
So, this is my conclusion,
only come find me Love when there is a Man worth pursuing
Goodbye Love
The back of me now is what you'll see moving

A SEATED STATE

She sits quietly surrounded my many
To her ears there is no sound
But blue skies without ending
She's dreamed of this her whole aching life
To live
Breathe
She dreamed of a glow shining brightly
To be seen
Heard
Felt
To feel again
So much hurt she has endured without mend
So many tears shed not just for others but her Sins
She has grown weary
Tired
And calls out for an end

She dreams of the wind carrying her away
Far beyond all she's known
Far beyond flesh and bone
What will this new journey bring
Will her first step be her new begin
She sits silently awaiting the take off
Soon all images of her past become empty
Unfortunately, a memory occasionally seeps back in

A CHILD'S TEMPTATION

Streetlights excite
as temptation of the night sends an invite,
A predator at most,
seeking the young as its next host
Angel child untouched by this poisonous air
unsure of what's clean,
being easy to manipulate,
eyes gleam from the shiny things
A life without substance was the cake baked

Parading about creating a spark
far away from upright
What will your pleasure be tonight
Drugs,
Sex,
Money,
Or the chase of fame
Follow me
I'll show in life there are no morals
just a stage to display the games we play
As fools thinking we are men
Ha,
I'll laugh at you trying to defend your point of view
If it's opposite of mine,
Don't you know majority rules?

The streetlights excited me
So, I walked head up proudly
Until one day truth came
But it was too late
As not even I,
could find me

COCAINE

Early morning quivers as I lay shaking my inner thighs
I require you
You, not just for your affect
But your copulating arousal
Shower me with your fairy powder
Your coca leaves orate to me
As you form into my admirable stimulant
I began abrading my body coveting in search of your arrival
 As we both know it is imminent
Without you my body descends as the twin towers
Please be my immediate first responder
Awaken me to a place of enchanting showers
with heighten sensors as my nerves actuate
a correlation of spasms
I'll taste you first
Then you taste mine
We will have this albino dust draped all over us
You have left your blemish of cocaine fever
Your drug to my skeleton acts as my transceiver
with me being graciously the receiver
There are no restrictions
With you I feel freer
My sinful addiction
As you play the overseer

GIRL LOST

Shameless girl,
Look at her sway into the night
Dress so fitted but her walk is far from upright
Swinging her hair from left to right
Careful now,
Don't want it to take flight

Unrecognizable face in a painted picture
Body sculpted and molded into a different figure
Each morning looking into a mirror sends a trigger buried deep within
Still defamed, feeling detained from a lost spirit within
Even that thousand-dollar designer bag wages sin

Shameless girl,
Tainted with illusions got you delusional chasing chills in the wind
Body in movement but your mind still stagnant
Stuck in a social media binge
The height of your fame is dancing in a pig's pen entrenched with others alike,
The unhinged always want friends

Shameless girl,
When will you learn your salvation will be the result of what is earned?
To one Father, all his children can be returned

A PLACE OF DESOLATE

Wasted land of a desolate place
Silence remains as the chairs rust away
What hidden treasures may live in a home decayed?
And behind its reach, lies a wooded place
What would be found on this path to take?
Will life be met where love once dwelt or
Withered pastures and trees unkempt
More brown than green I see before me
Yet, the sun brightens the sky over its height
Then once again it is filled with a darkened plight
The wind blows silently here
And voices whisper in the night
I envision two lovers seated at the table pulled away from one another in spite
The last of them
The last who knew
What stories this tree would tell, the one of many roots
What once begat here with life anew
Oh! barren place I cry out to you
For you are much like me, a woman with an empty womb

NOT ANOTHER STATISTIC

There
are fists banging on the walls
with siren sounds,
blood stains and
rivers of tears
Her baby's gone
If only she had another year
What bright faces
And honorable mentions
She was top student of the year
Then topped off
I mean head popped off
From a shiny piece of silver
Black is the ugliest color of them all
This is the last day
I mean the last time I put this on
Wet faces around me
Sweet talk of a prodigy who once lived
But is now gone
No! You can't have her
Give her back
To me and others around,
she still matters
I've suffered way too long
Daddy drunk up a stunk
Soon after, I became his drum
Momma thirsting for her next rush
"Mr. Please, I'll do anything"
Grandma strongest of us all
Yet,

Still scraping pennies
for our next meal
Can't take the edge off
I'll take anything

Any pill
Uncle smiling at me
"What pretty girl you have become"
Gotta run
Have to hide
Before all innocence soon have died
Please!
Somebody Help!
I am human
Hear my cry

UNSETTLED

My spirit is restless
Despite all of my efforts,
some of which were reckless,
I am not in hopes of where I started
Escaping is all I imagine
From you, from me, from life
Sometimes I can see a grand scheme
But it is later revealed to me that in life nothing is at it seems

Do I smile just to make peace
Hide until I discover me OR
Cry a sour taste because that is what living seems to be
I feel my best when the sun covers me
Together we melt away as one without need for anything
I hear heartbeats of life among the gardens around me
Trace the images of seas and oceans within my mind
Yet, I wander about,
still lost—unfound
Making the same old mistakes a thousand times
My spirit is quiet but screams so loudly
As I await the day where I can see a different me,
Proudly

I LOVE AND HATE MY HAIR

The best part is when my morning fingers twirl between each coil
Coarse threads that carry strength
Yet, delicately soft and can shrivel away if not properly cared for
Prepping and priming with hours in
Still unflattering
Left hidden by weaves and wigs
Maybe one day, someday me and my hair will be friends

I love the glow it carries fresh out of the shower
The unique shapes and patterns that others with straight hair try to acquire
I think today I'll pack in product
Let the world see me naturally in hopes to inspire
But Unkind looks and whispers left me feeling un-bloomed as the death of a flower

I love the difference it holds but hate the indifferences it brings
What shall I do?
I was made to have hair this way
As I stand in front of a mirror and stare
I'll look into it and admire what is there
Still screaming the same notions of how I love and hate my hair

GLIDE JELLY BEAN GLIDE

They tell you,
you are a nuisance,
you are the gum latched to a shoe
that they have to annoyingly pick away
You smile back with a face of
reverence
Not of translucence
but opaque
as your walk is of the
benevolence
Head high
but spirit higher
where there is no greater peek

Inaudibly,
you trace invisible steps forward that no other can see
Faces frown while eyes roll
but gardens outshine in a world of colors, mostly green

You walk without shame or pride
Humbleness is your strength-untied
Glide Jelly Bean Glide
Smooth in motion
with each stride
Dispute hate as they
stand frozen and
watch as you rise

FINDING BEAUTY

It took some time for me to get acquainted with I
To learn to undie
To embrace my flaws
Remove all negative thoughts without pause
And channel my inner beauty
Realizing accepting me was my duty

Unsure of how to go about it
So my cries went into his holy writ
Re-training my spirit to recommit
Removing the hatred of oneself, the original sin
I have now found beauty within my skin
A love in depth and far from thin

TIMELESS DREAM

I am lost abound with you in my mind
Who are you?
This is a light I have never seen shine
I could almost smell you
See your smile from far away
I imagine my life with you all the time
And the way we wine
You must be my forever
I can release the darkened parts of me and you stay without running and fix the incomplete parts of me
Raw honey we make
I am certain that there would never be a mistake of misleading or manipulation
As we are both elevated enough to begin a pure creation
But where are you Love
Right now you are every bit of my dream
Maybe one day love
we'll meet and you'll start my heartbeat

HE KISSES MY ACNE

How I know his love is real
He is attentive beyond my needs
He vocalizes to me spiritually
Awaking passions long buried deep
When face to face with the heart of me
He embraces me quietly as he kisses my acne

I love the tone his voice carries
Adamant yet benevolently admitting power
He gives me a love of many showers
To others our bond seems uncanny
I say nothing about us is aptly
As he lowers his head I breath out as he kisses my acne

What better heartbeat for me to surrender
From January through December,
 I am his center and he my defender
Did you catch that analogy
I said everyday with him is a grand finale
I love the way he catches me as I fall in depth
To him I give the best of me
because he,
kisses my acne

A MIND THAT SOON SLEEPS

The mind waits for no one as it deteriorates.
We smile today knowing but tomorrow our expressions are blank.
Our minds repeat old memories but for the current ones it draws a line.
What is of true reality?
What is real vs fake?
I can sometimes see images tucked away in my hippocampus and
there they'll stay until they too become a blank canvas.
This agony of awaiting as I silently slip away,
praying so continuously until I soon forget the days.

REMEMBER ME

Remember me not for my textured hair
and divergent features
Not for my buxom build or legs that roared in 6-inch heels
Remember me not as a simple mind as I am such of a complex
    creature
Not for my darkened skin or ample nose
But remember me as life unlike an object that does not feel
For I am more in all my glory as a single rose

Remember my laughter and the wetness of my tears
Remember my climb on courageous heights carrying life's fears
Remember my voice and how loudly it rang with passionate empathy
for all things clean
Remember my walk towards light upright
But remember my pain that once burdened me when I lived ashamed
Remember my face seen as the human race
Remember that each breath given is time of pure grace

Jenquia Jamison is a self-taught southern native poet, illustrator, and acrylic painter from New Orleans, LA currently residing in Indianapolis, IN. Growing up in her home with two siblings, creative arts has always been a hidden pleasure of hers. She would often find herself surrounded by nature's arms while eluded from the outside world, adrift within her imagination creating some form of art. Having the support of her loving parents gave her the courage to live within her passions which has never negated her.

Her home usually consists of one or more fury friends and she has a deep love for animals. Throughout her life, her field of work has always been helping others consisting of working as a Vet Assistant after achieving her associate's degree in veterinary medicine, assisting the elderly and those suffering with mental illness and addiction. Jenquia's love for inspiring and helping others is what gives her purpose.

Because she was able to grow up in such a brightly colored city full of inspiration from majestic sceneries, music, local cuisine to cultural celebrations, and dance has allowed her to find a deeper beauty within life. She believes we are all here to appreciate, create, advocate, and cultivate by means of visual and verbal expression. Her goal is to indeed plant her seeds into the world.

During her duration of writing, she has published poetry through the Poetry Society of Indiana in an anthology titled; "Ink to Paper" Vol 5 and with Sidney & Lois Eskenazi Hospital in "Eskenazi Heath Cares" Vol 8 Issue 4. This goes not without a few honorable mentions on other pieces.

Writing and painting is her release of agony along with memorable beauty stuck within her mind. Her voice is not just for herself, but all other voices that have been silenced.

www.ingramcontent.com/pod-product-compliance
Lightning Source LLC
Chambersburg PA
CBHW022127090426
42743CB00008B/1038